IMPRINT: Independently published

I0446682

TABLE OF CONTENTS

INTRODUCTION

What is Forex Trading? A Beginners Guide.

Forex (FX) is a combination of the phrases foreign [currency] and exchange. Foreign exchange is the practice of converting one currency into another for different purposes, mainly for trade, trading, or tourism. According to a 2022 triennial report from the Bank for International Settlements (a worldwide bank for national central banks), the daily global volume for currency trading hit $7.5 trillion in 2022. Read on to understand about the forex markets, what they're used for, and how to start trading.

The foreign exchange (forex or FX) market is a worldwide marketplace for exchanging national currencies. Because of the international spread of trade, business, and finance, FX markets tend to be the world's biggest and most liquid asset markets. Currencies trade against one other as exchange rate pairings. For example, EUR/USD is a currency pair for trading the euro against the U.S. dollar. Forex markets operate as spot (cash) and derivatives markets, including forwards, futures, options, and currency swaps. Some market players utilize forex to hedge against international currency and interest rate risk, speculate on geopolitical events, and diversify portfolios, among other reasons.

What Is the Forex Market? A Beginner's Guide

The foreign exchange market is where currencies are exchanged. This worldwide market's most distinctive attribute is that it lacks a central marketplace. Instead, currency trading is handled electronically over the counter (OTC). This implies that all transactions occur over computer networks among dealers globally rather than on one controlled exchange.

The market is open 24 hours a day, five and a half days a week. Currencies are traded internationally in the main financial capitals of Frankfurt, Hong Kong, London, New York, Paris, Singapore, Sydney, Tokyo, and Zurich—across practically every time zone. This implies the forex market opens in Tokyo and Hong Kong after the U.S. trading day concludes. As such, the currency market may be very busy at any moment, with price quotations changing regularly. You'll commonly encounter the phrases FX, forex, foreign exchange market, and currency market. These concepts are equivalent, and all pertain to the FX market.

CHAPTER [1]

How Does the Forex Market Work?

The FX market is the only really continuous and constant trading market in the world. In the past, the forex market was controlled by institutional corporations and huge banks, that operated on behalf of customers. But it has grown increasingly retail-oriented in recent years—traders and investors of all sizes engage in it.

Where Is It?

An unusual element of international forex markets is that no physical structures operate as trading venues. Instead, it is a system of linked trade terminals and computer networks. Market players include institutions, investment banks, commercial banks, and individual investors from throughout the globe.

Who Trades on It?

Currency trading was highly difficult for private investors before it found its way onto the internet. Most currency traders were major multinational organizations, hedge funds, or high-net-worth individuals (HNWIs) since forex trading needed a lot of cash. Commercial and investment banks still do most of the trading in FX markets on behalf of their customers. But there are also chances for professional and ordinary investors to trade one currency against another.

<u>Types of Markets</u>

Forex is traded largely through spot, forward, and futures markets. The spot market is the biggest of all three markets since it is the "underlying" asset on which forwards and futures markets are based. When individuals speak about the forex market, they are typically talking about the spot market. The forwards and futures markets tend to be more popular with corporations or financial institutions that need to hedge their foreign currency risks out to a certain future date.

Spot Market

The spot market is where currencies are purchased and sold depending on their trading price. That price is decided by supply and demand and is estimated depending on numerous criteria, such as:

- Current interest rates
- Economic performance
- Geopolitical sentiment
- Price speculation

A concluded agreement on the spot market is known as a spot deal. It is a bilateral transaction in which one party provides an agreed-upon currency quantity to the counterparty and gets a defined amount of another currency at the agreed-upon exchange rate value. After a position is closed, it is paid in cash. Although the spot market is typically characterized as one that deals with transactions in the now (rather than in the future), these trades require two days to settle.

Forwards and Futures Markets

A forward contract is a private agreement between two parties to acquire a currency at a future date at a set price in the OTC markets. In the forwards market, contracts are purchased and sold OTC between two parties, who set the terms of the arrangement between themselves.

A futures contract is a standardized agreement between two parties to take delivery of a currency at a future date and a defined price. Futures trade on exchanges and not OTC. In the futures market, futures contracts are purchased and sold based on a specified size and settlement date on public commodities marketplaces, such as the Chicago Mercantile Exchange (CME).

Futures contracts feature precise characteristics, such as the number of units being traded, delivery and settlement dates, and minimum price increments that cannot be altered. The exchange works as a counterparty to the trader, offering clearing and settlement services.

Unlike the spot, forwards, and futures markets, the options market does not exchange physical currencies. Instead, it trades in contracts that indicate claims to a given currency type, a specified price per unit, and a future date for settlement.

Both forms of contracts are binding and are normally settled for cash at the exchange in question upon expiration, but contracts may also be purchased and sold before they expire. These markets may give protection against risk when trading currencies.

In addition to forwards and futures, options contracts are traded on particular currency pairings. currency options provide investors the right, but not the duty, to engage in a currency deal at a future date.

Using the Forex Markets

There are two different properties of currencies as an asset class:

You may earn the interest rate discrepancy between two currencies. You may benefit from fluctuations in the currency rate. So, you may benefit from the difference between two interest rates in two separate economies by purchasing the currency with the higher interest rate and shorting the currency with the lower interest rate. For instance, before the 2008 financial crisis, shorting the Japanese yen (JPY) and purchasing British pounds (GBP) was prevalent since the interest rate disparity was considerable. This method is also referred to as a carry trade.

Forex for Hedging

Companies conducting business in other nations are at risk owing to swings in currency values when they acquire or sell products and services outside of their home market. Foreign exchange markets give a mechanism to hedge currency risk by establishing a rate at which the transaction will be executed. A trader may purchase or sell currencies in the forward or swap markets in advance, which locks in an exchange rate.

Locking in the exchange rate helps them minimize losses or raise earnings, depending on whether the currency in a pair is strengthened or weakened.

Forex for Speculation

Factors including interest rates, trade flows, tourism, economic strength, and geopolitical risk impact the supply and demand for currencies, producing daily volatility in the currency markets. This gives possibilities to benefit from developments that may boost or diminish one currency's value relative to another. A prognosis that one currency will decline is basically the same as expecting that the other currency in the pair would rise.

So, a trader expecting price movement might short or long one of the currencies in a pair and take advantage of the fluctuation.

How to Start Trading Forex

Trading FX is comparable to stock trading. Here are some tips to get yourself started on the forex trading path.

Learn about forex: While it is not complex, forex trading is an endeavor that demands specific knowledge and a dedication to study.

Set up a brokerage account: You will need a forex trading account with a brokerage to get started with forex trading.

Develop a trading plan: While it is not always feasible to foresee and time market movement, having a trading strategy can help you define broad principles and a road map for trading.

Always be on top of your numbers: Once you begin trading, review your positions at the end of the day. Most trading software currently gives a daily accounting of deals. execute sure that you do not have any outstanding positions to be filled and that you have adequate funds in your account to execute future transactions.

Cultivate emotional equilibrium: Beginner forex trading is riddled with emotional roller coasters and unresolved issues. Discipline yourself to close out your positions when required.

Forex Terminology

The easiest approach to get started on the forex adventure is to understand its language. Here are a few terms to get you started:

- Forex account: A forex account is used to perform currency trading. Depending on the lot size, there may be three kinds of FX accounts:

- Micro forex accounts: Accounts that enable you to trade up to $1,000 worth of currencies in one lot.

- Mini forex accounts: Accounts that enable you to trade up to $10,000 worth of currencies in one lot.

- Standard forex accounts: Accounts that enable you to trade up to $100,000 worth of currencies in one lot.

- Ask: An ask (or offer) is the lowest price at which you are willing to acquire a currency.

- Bid: A bid is the price at which you are ready to sell a currency.

- Contract for difference: A contract for difference (CFD) is a derivative that enables traders to speculate on price changes for currencies without owning the underlying asset.

- Leverage: Leverage is employing borrowed money to multiply profits. The forex market is characterized by huge leverages, and traders typically utilize it to strengthen their holdings. Remember that the trading limit for each lot includes margin money utilized for leverage. This implies the broker may give you with funds in a predefined ratio. For example, they may put up $50 for every $1 you put up for trading, meaning you will only need to utilize $10 from your savings to swap $500 in cash.

Basic Forex Trading Strategies

The most fundamental kinds of forex transactions are long and short trades. In a long transaction, the trader is wagering that the currency price will climb and that they can benefit from it. A short trade consists of a wager that the currency pair's price will decline. Traders may also utilize trading methods based on technical analysis, such as breakout and moving averages, to fine-tune their approach to trade.

Depending on the length and quantities for trading, trading methods may be split into four additional types:

- Scalp Trade: A scalp trade consists of cumulative positions maintained for seconds or minutes at most, and the profit amounts are confined in terms of the number of pips.

- Day Trade: Day trades are short-term transactions in which holdings are held and liquidated on the same day. The period of a day trade might be hours or minutes.

- Swing Trade: In a swing trade, the trader keeps the position for a time longer than a day, such as days or weeks.

- Position Transaction: In a position transaction, the trader keeps the currency for a lengthy term, lasting as long as months or even years.

Charts Used in Forex Trading

Three kinds of charts are utilized in forex trading. They are:

Line Charts

Line charts are used to detect big-picture patterns for a currency. They are the most basic and ubiquitous sort of chart utilized by forex traders. They show the closing trading price for a currency for the periods provided by the user. The trend lines found in a line chart may be utilized to design trading strategies. For example, you may utilize the information in a trend line to spot breakouts or a shift in trend for increasing or dropping prices. While informative, a line chart is often used as a starting point for additional trading research.

Bar Charts

Like other cases in which they are employed, bar charts give more pricing information than line charts. Each bar chart represents one day of trading and covers the opening price, highest price, lowest price, and closing price (OHLC) for a transaction. A dash on the left symbolizes the day's beginning price, while a similar one on the right represents the closing price. Colors are occasionally used to signify price fluctuation, with green or white used for periods of increasing prices and red or black for a period during which prices decreased. Bar charts for currency trading assist traders to assess if it is a buyer's or seller's market.

Candlestick Charts

Japanese rice dealers originally employed candlestick charts in the 18th century. They are aesthetically more attractive and simpler to read than the chart kinds discussed above. The top section of a candle is utilized for the starting price and greatest price point of a currency, while the bottom half denotes the closing price and lowest price point. A down candle is a time of dropping prices and is tinted red or black, whereas an up candle shows a period of growing prices and is shaded green or white.

The forms and shapes of candlestick charts are used to detect market direction and movement. Some of the most typical forms for candlestick charts include hanging man and shooting star.

<u>Pros</u>

Forex markets are the biggest in terms of daily trading volume internationally and consequently provide the greatest liquidity.

This makes it possible to join and exit a trade in any major currency within a fraction of a second for a tiny spread in most market situations.

The currency market is traded 24 hours a day, five and a half days a week—starting each day in Australia and concluding in New York. The large time horizon and coverage provide traders with an opportunity to generate gains or cover losses. The biggest forex market centers arc Frankfurt, Hong Kong, London, New York, Paris, Singapore, Sydney, Tokyo, and Zurich.

The available leverage in forex trading implies that a trader's initial capital may quickly grow.

Forex trading normally follows the same laws as ordinary trading and needs considerably less initial money; consequently, it is simpler to start trading forex than stocks. The currency market is more decentralized than conventional stock or bond markets. There is no centralized exchange that controls currency transaction activities, and the possibility for manipulation—through insider knowledge about a firm or stock—is smaller.

<u>Cons</u>

Leveraged trading may make forex deals substantially more volatile than trading without leverage.

Banks, brokers, and dealers in the forex markets enable a significant degree of leverage, meaning traders may manage enormous positions with very little money.

Leverage in the region of 50:1 is normal in forex, while even larger degrees of leverage are available from specific brokers. Nevertheless, leverage must be handled judiciously since many rookie traders have incurred big losses employing greater leverage than was required or practical. Trading currencies successfully demands an awareness of economic principles and indicators. A currency trader has to have a big-picture knowledge of the economies of many nations and their interconnectivity to appreciate the fundamentals that determine currency prices.

The decentralized structure of FX markets means it is less regulated than other financial markets. The amount and form of regulation in forex markets depend on the trading jurisdiction.

Forex markets lack tools that generate continuous income, such as monthly dividend payments, which would make them appealing to investors not interested in exponential returns.

Are Forex Markets Volatile?

Forex markets are among the most liquid marketplaces in the world. So, they may be less volatile than other markets, such as real estate. The volatility of a given currency is a product of various variables, such as the politics and economy of its nation. Therefore, events like economic instability in the form of a payment failure or imbalance in trade connections with another currency may result in severe volatility.

Are Forex Markets Regulated?

Forex trading legislation varies on the jurisdiction. Countries like the United States have sophisticated infrastructure and marketplaces for FX transactions. Forex trading is heavily regulated in the U.S. by the National Futures Association (NFA) and the Commodity Futures Trading Commission (CFTC). However, owing to the large use of leverage in forex transactions, emerging nations like India and China impose limits on the businesses and money to be utilized in forex trading. Europe is the biggest market for FX transactions. The Financial Conduct Authority (FCA) supervises and regulates currency trading in the United Kingdom.

Which Currencies Can I Trade in?

Currencies with high liquidity have a ready market and demonstrate smooth and predictable price activity in reaction to external events. The U.S. dollar is the most traded currency in the world. It is matched up in six of the market's seven most liquid currency pairings. Currencies with little liquidity, however, cannot be traded in high lot sizes without considerable market movement being connected with the price.

The Bottom Line

For traders—especially those with little funds—day trading or swing trading in small quantities is simpler in the FX market than in other marketplaces. For individuals with longer-term goals and greater finances, long-term fundamentals-based trading or a carry trade may be beneficial. An emphasis on understanding the macroeconomic fundamentals that drive currency prices, as well as familiarity with technical analysis, may help novice forex traders become more lucrative.

CHAPTER [2]

Foreign Exchange Market

The foreign exchange market (forex, FX, or currency market) is a worldwide decentralized or over-the-counter (OTC) market for the trading of currencies. This market establishes foreign exchange rates for every currency. It comprises all elements of purchasing, selling, and exchanging currencies at current or set values. In terms of trade volume, it is by far the biggest market in the world, followed by the credit market.

- US Dollar Index DXY
- US Dollar Index (DXY)

- USD/GBP exchange rate
- USD/Canadian dollar conversion rate
- EUR/USD (inverted) exchange rate
- USD/JPY exchange rate
- USD/SEK exchange rate
- USD/CHF exchange rate

The key players in this sector are the big multinational banks. Financial hubs across the globe act as anchors of trade between a broad variety of diverse sorts of buyers and sellers around the clock, with the exception of weekends. Since currencies are usually exchanged in pairs, the foreign exchange market does not define a currency's absolute value but rather sets its relative worth by determining the market price of one currency if paid for with another. Ex: 1 USD is worth X CAD, or CHF, or JPY, etc.

The foreign exchange market works via financial institutions and operates on numerous levels. Behind the scenes, banks turn to a smaller number of financial organizations known as "dealers", who are engaged in substantial volumes of foreign currency trading. Most foreign currency traders are banks, therefore this behind-the-scenes market is frequently termed the "interbank market" (although a few insurance companies and other sorts of financial institutions are engaged). Trades between foreign currency brokers may be quite big, involving hundreds of millions of dollars. Because of the sovereignty problem when involving two currencies, Forex has limited (if any) supervisory authority controlling its conduct.

The foreign exchange market promotes international commerce and investments by permitting currency conversion. For example, it lets a firm in the United States buy items from European Union member states, particularly Eurozone members, and pay Euros, even if its revenue is in United States dollars. It also enables direct speculation and assessment relative to the value of currencies and the carry trade speculation, based on the differential interest rate between two currencies.

In a typical foreign exchange transaction, a party purchases some quantity of one currency by paying with some quantity of another currency.

The current foreign exchange market started emerging throughout the 1970s. This followed three decades of government limitations on foreign currency transactions under the Bretton Woods system of monetary management, which laid out the rules for commercial and financial dealings among the world's main industrial governments following World War II. Countries progressively shifted to floating exchange rates from the previous currency rate regime, which remained set per the Bretton Woods arrangement.

The foreign exchange market is distinctive because of the following characteristics:

- Its vast trading volume, constituting the biggest asset class in the world contributing to high liquidity;

- Its geographical dispersal;

- Its continuous operation: 24 hours a day save for weekends, i.e., trading from 22:00 UTC on Sunday

(Sydney) through 22:00 UTC on Friday (New York);

- The range of variables that determine exchange rates;

- The low margins of relative profit compared with other markets of fixed income; and

- The use of leverage to boost profit and loss margins and with regard to account size.

As such, it has been characterized as the market closest to the ideal of complete competition, ignoring currency intervention by central banks. According to the Bank for International Settlements, the preliminary worldwide figures from the 2022 Triennial Central Bank Survey of Foreign Exchange and

OTC Derivatives Markets Activity reveal that trade in foreign exchange markets averaged US$7.5 trillion per day in April 2022. This is up from US$6.6 trillion in April 2019. Measured by value, foreign currency swaps were traded more than any other instrument in April 2022, at US$3.8 trillion per day, followed by spot trading at US$2.1 trillion.[3]

The $7.5 trillion break-down is as follows:

$2.1 trillion in spot trades
$1.2 trillion in outright forwards
$3.8 trillion in foreign exchange swaps
$124 billion currency swaps
$304 billion in options and other items

CHAPTER [3]

FOREX TRADING: WHAT IS FOREX?

Forex trading is a phrase used to describe persons that are involved in the active exchange of foreign currencies, generally for the aim of financial profit or gain. That may take on the shape of speculators, who are trying to purchase or sell a currency with the purpose of gaining from the currency's price movement; or it might be a hedger that's attempting to safeguard their accounts in the case of an unfavorable move against their currency holdings.

The phrase 'forex trader' may indicate an individual trader on a retail platform, a bank trader employing an institutional platform, or hedgers who may be either managing their own risk or outsourcing that role to a bank or money manager to manage the risk for them.

FOREX TRADING: THE FX MARKET

The foreign exchange market, or forex (FX) for short, is a decentralized marketplace that allows the buying and selling of various currencies. This is done over the counter (OTC) instead of on a controlled exchange.

Without knowing it, you have probably already engaged in the foreign exchange market by purchasing imported things such as apparel or shoes, or more overtly, buying foreign money while on vacation. Traders may be lured to forex for numerous reasons, including:

- The size of the FX market

- A vast choice of currencies to trade

- Differing degrees of volatility

- Low transaction costs

- 24 hours a day trading throughout the week

This book will target traders of all levels. Whether you are fresh new to forex trading or want to improve on your previous expertise, this book strives to give a firm foundation to the foreign exchange market.

FOREX TRADING: TWO SIDES OF EVERY MARKET

One distinctive characteristic of the Forex market is the method by which prices are stated. Because currencies form the bedrock of the financial system, the only way to quote a currency is by utilizing other currencies. This generates a relative value gauge that may seem perplexing at first but may become more normalized the longer that one works with this two-sided convention.

Forex trading in a pair does provide the trader a little of extra freedom, by enabling the trader or investor the chance to speak their transaction against the currency that they consider most suitable.

Let's take the Euro for example, and let's suppose a trader has bullish expectations for the European economy and would thusly prefer to become the currency. But let's imagine this investor is likewise optimistic for the US economy but pessimistic for the UK economy. Well, in this case, the investor isn't obligated to purchase the Euro against the US Dollar (which would be a long EUR/USD trade); and they may, instead, buy the Euro against the British Pound (going long EUR/GBP).

This provides the investor or trader that additional bit of flexibility, enabling them to avoid 'going short' the US Dollar to purchase the Euro and, instead, allowing them to buy the Euro while going short the British Pound.

FOREX TRADING: BASE V/S COUNTER CURRENCIES

One key characteristic of a Forex quotation is the convention: The first currency included in the quotation is known as the 'base' currency of the pair, and this is the asset that's being quoted. The second currency in the pair is known as the 'counter' currency, and this is the convention of the quotation or the currency that's being used to describe the value of the first currency in the pair.

LET'S TAKE EUR/USD AS AN EXAMPLE...

The Euro is the first currency in the quotation, therefore the Euro would be the base currency in the EUR/USD currency pair.

The US Dollar is the second currency in the quotation, and this is the currency that the EUR/USD quote is utilizing to establish the value of the Euro.

So, let's imagine that the EUR/USD quotation is 1.3000. That would imply that 1 Euro is worth $1.30. If the price rises up to $1.35 – then the Euro would have grown in value and, on a relative basis, the US Dollar would've declined in value.

If an investor was bearish on the Euro but bullish on the US Dollar, they might opt to 'short' the pair, anticipating prices to fall; after which they could 'cover' the bet by purchasing it back at a lower price, and pocketing the difference.

FOREX TRADING: THE FOREX MARKET EXPLAINED

In a word, the foreign currency market functions like many other markets in that it's driven by supply and demand. Using a very simple example, if there is a huge demand for the US Dollar from European people holding Euros, they will trade their Euros into Dollars. The value of the US Dollar will grow while the value of the Euro will plummet. Keep in mind that this transaction solely impacts the EUR/USD currency combination and will not, for example, cause the USD to devalue against the Japanese Yen.

FOREX TRADING: WHAT DRIVES THE FLOWS?

In actuality, the aforementioned example is merely one of many variables that may impact the FX market. Others include broad macro-economic events like the election of a new president, or nation-specific elements such as the prevailing interest rate, GDP, unemployment, inflation, and the debt to GDP ratio, to mention a few. Top traders make use of an economic calendar to remain up to speed with these and other major data announcements that might impact the market.

On a longer-term basis, one important driver of Forex prices is interest rates from the connected economy, since this may have a direct influence on holding a currency either long or short.

WHAT EXPLAINS THE POPULARITY?

The foreign exchange market enables huge institutions, governments, retail traders, and private people to swap one currency for another and the 'core' of the FX market is what's known as the interbank market, which is where liquidity providers trade amongst each other.

The advantage of having forex trading between global banks and liquidity providers is that forex may be traded around the clock (during the week). As the trading day in Asia draws to a close, the European and UK banks come online before turning over to the US. The whole trading day concludes when the US session leads into the Asian session for the following day.

What makes this market even more interesting to traders is The around-the-clock liquidity that is typically accessible. This implies that traders may readily join and exit positions since there are many ready buyers and sellers for foreign currency.

FOREX TRADING: HOW DOES IT WORK?

This is fairly similar to other markets: If you believe the value of a currency is likely to go up (appreciate), you might seek to purchase the currency. This is known as going "long". If you sense the currency is likely to go down (depreciate), you sell that currency. This is described as becoming "short".

FOREX TRADING: WHO ARE THE MAJOR PLAYERS?

There are basically two sorts of traders in the foreign currency market: hedgers and speculators. Hedgers are continually attempting to prevent large swings in the currency rate. Think about huge businesses like Exxon and how they strive to minimize their exposure to international currency volatility.

Speculators, on the other hand, are risk-hungry and constantly searching for volatility in exchange rates to take advantage of. These include massive trading desks at the main banks and retail traders.

READING A FOREX QUOTE

All traders need to grasp how to read a forex quotation since this will decide the price you enter and exit the deal. Looking at the currency quotation below, the first currency in the EUR/USD pair is known as the base currency, which is the Euro, while the second currency in this combination (the USD) is known as the variable or quote currency.

For most FX markets, prices are provided up to five decimals but the first four are the most relevant. The number to the left of the decimal point denotes one unit of the counter currency, in this example, it is the USD and so is $1. The next two numbers are the cents, thus in this example 13 US cents. The third and fourth numbers indicate fractions of a cent and are referred to as pips.

It's crucial to remember that the number at the fourth decimal place is known as a 'pip'. Should the EUR drop against the USD by 100 pips, the new sell price will reflect the lower price of 1.12528 since it will cost less in USD to acquire 1 Euro. Another method of stating the above-reported bid price is that the value of One Euro, in terms of US Dollars, is One Dollar, 13 cents, 52 pips, and 8/10th of a pip.

<u>WHAT IS A 'PIP'?</u>

Pip stands for 'percentage in point,' and this is the foundation unit of measurement in a currency pair. The value of a pip will change depending on the counter-currency in the pairing. For currency pairings in which USD is the counter-currency, or stated second in the quotation, the pip value or cost will frequently be $1 for a 10k lot of currency, which would also imply a pip value or cost of 10 cents for a 1k lot and $10.00 for a 100k lot.

So, if an investor buys a 1k lot of EUR/USD, each pip gained or lost would be worth 10 cents. If the same investor buys a 10k lot of EUR/USD, each pip gained or lost would be worth $1/each. And if the investor buys a 100k lot, the pip value would be $10/per.

Running with this example: Let's imagine that the investor who purchased EUR/USD received a 50 pip gain. Well, if the investor was using a 1k lot, the 50 pip gain would equate to $5 ($.10 X 50 = 5.00); while an investor using a 10k lot would have a gain of $50 ($1 x 50 = $50). And if the same investor was dealing with a 100k lot, the gain would be $500 ($10.00 x 50 = $500).

Pip cost or value are incredibly significant data items for forex traders to be aware of since this is how spreads are conveyed; hence is very crucial for traders to 'know their pips.'

FOREX TRADING ON DEMO ACCOUNTS: GAINING EXPERIENCE WITHOUT RISKING HARD CAPITAL

One of the major hazards or negatives of learning a market or learning to trade is the fact that trading can be an expensive effort, and the potential for financial loss is ever-present when trading real hard cash on a trading platform. Whenever one buys or sells a Forex pair, they run the chance of losing money, and for a beginner trader who's just learning their skills, this may be a costly tuition.

However many Forex brokers provide demo accounts so that novice traders or potential clients may familiarize themselves with the market, the platform, and the mechanics of forex trading before ever depositing a Dollar, Euro, or Pound of their own money.

The demo account may give a virtual environment where a novice trader can execute their ideas and handle their transactions with fictitious cash. This may be a perfect location to understand the mechanics of forex trading - how to trigger positions, how to create stops, and how to scale out of deals.

FOREX TRADING: WHY TRADE FOREX?

Trading FX has various benefits over other markets as described below:

- Low transaction costs: Typically, forex brokers earn their money on the spread provided the deal is opened and finished before any overnight financing charges are imposed. Therefore, forex trading is cost-efficient when measured up against market-like shares, which bear a commission fee.

- Low spreads: Bid/Ask spreads are exceptionally low for key FX pairings owing to their liquidity. When trading, the spread is the first obstacle that has to be crossed when the market advances in your favor. Any more pips that shift in your favor is pure profit.

- More possibilities to profit: Forex trading enables traders to take speculative bets on currencies going up (appreciating) and going down (depreciating). Furthermore, there are many alternative currency pairings for traders to detect lucrative transactions.

- Leverage trading: Trading forex requires the use of leverage. This implies that a trader need not pay the whole cost of the deal but instead simply put down a part of the cost. This has the ability to amplify your earnings but also your losses. At DailyFX we advocate a systematic approach to risk management by keeping your effective leverage to 10 to one or less.

KEY FOREX TRADING TERMS

- Base currency: This is the initial currency that appears when quoting a currency pair. Looking at EUR/USD, the Euro is the base currency.

- Variable/quote currency: This is the second currency in the quoted currency pair and is the US Dollar in the EUR/USD example.

- Bid: The bid price is the maximum amount that a buyer (bidder) is willing to pay. When you are trying to sell a currency pair this is the price you will see, generally to the left of the quotation, and is commonly in red.

- Ask: This is the reverse of the bid and shows the lowest price a seller is ready to take. When you are trying to purchase a currency pair, this is the price you will see, and is normally on the right and in blue.

- Spread: This is the difference between the bid and the asking price which indicates the real spread in the underlying forex market plus the extra spread applied by the broker.

- Pips/points: A pip or point refers to a one-digit change in the 4th decimal place. This is generally how traders refer to moves in a currency pair, i.e. GBP/USD rallied 100 points today.

- Leverage: Leverage enables traders to trade positions while only putting up a percentage of the entire value of the deal. This permits traders to hold greater positions with a modest quantity of cash. Leverage multiplies earnings AND losses.

- Margin: This is the amount of money required to start a leveraged position and is the difference between the entire value of your position and the cash being given to you by the broker.

- Margin call: When the entire capital deposited, plus or minus any gains or losses, goes below a certain threshold (margin requirement).

- Liquidity: A currency pair is regarded to be liquid if it can readily be purchased and sold owing to numerous participants being trading the currency pair.

FREE RESOURCES AND GUIDES TO LEARN FOREX TRADING

If you are just starting out on your trading adventure it is crucial to grasp the fundamentals of forex trading in our free new to forex trading tutorial.

We also provide a choice of trading guides to boost your forex knowledge and strategy building. Our research team studied over 30 million live transactions to find the qualities of successful traders. Incorporate these attributes to offer oneself an advantage in the marketplace. Traders typically look to retail customer mood while trading major FX markets.

DailyFX offers similar statistics, based on IG client sentiment.

FOREX TRADING FREQUENTLY ASKED QUESTIONS (FAQ)

What is Forex Trading?

Forex trading is the act of exchanging one currency for another. The way in which currency values are published lends itself to trading possibilities since each currency is priced in terms of other currencies. The Euro may be quoted against the US Dollar (EUR/USD), the British Pound (EUR/GBP), and the Japanese Yen (EUR/JPY) amongst several other currencies providing a large list of EUR-pairings accessible to traders.

Why do individuals trade Forex?

The most typical explanation here would be that people trade Forex with the purpose of generating profits, by purchasing a currency 'low' and then selling 'high,' or vice versa with short positions in which the goal would be to 'sell high' and 'cover lower.'

But this doesn't explain the intentions of all Forex traders, since many 'hedgers' or institutions are only attempting to ease risk against unfavorable currency moves against their positions or investments. An example of this may be an international corporation like Toyota, trying to eliminate or hedge a part of their exposure in the Yen. Otherwise, if Toyota was entirely invested in the Yen through their capital reserves, and the Yen weakened in value, Toyota's primary business could be vulnerable to the currency losses in the portfolio; and this is a risk that can be addressed through diversifying or hedging their currency position.

How can someone get started in Forex trading?

A smart initial step would be to acquaint oneself with the mechanics of the market using a demo account, which may enable a beginner trader to take on positions and manage their exposure with fictitious cash in a simulated environment. The trial account may provide the potential Forex trader the chance to trade in a simulated environment without the danger of financial loss.

This may be a great training ground for novice traders to discover the mechanics of Forex trading while creating their techniques and having a better notion of how they want to approach the market for themselves.

What is the 'best' approach to go about Forex Trading?

There isn't one generally appreciated approach that traders may use that's head and shoulders above the others. For most FX traders, the key is determining what works for them, and that's typically based on their own personalities or world views. Probably one of the most relevant expressions surrounding this subject is that there's not just one technique to go about trading Forex: There are short-term traders who watch their positions on five-minute charts and there are long-term traders who may not glance at pricing but once a day.

If you're hoping to gain a better sense of what may fit for you, the DailyFX DNA FX quiz might help: It's a 14-question personality test meant to give you an idea of what the ideal strategy may be for someone of a similar personality type. You may click the link below to begin the quiz, following which you'll be presented with your 'trader type' depending on the answers you have provided.

Becoming a forex trader means living and breathing the thrill, danger, and reward of trading in the largest and most liquid market in the world. Do you have what it takes? In this essay we'll discuss how you can become a forex trader, showing the attributes you need and the steps to take to get started and be a consistent trader.

WHAT DOES A FOREX TRADER DO?

A forex trader takes long or short bets on currency pairs with the purpose of generating a profit. A forex trader is strategic, disciplined, and constantly turned on to the markets. Whether focusing on a technical or fundamental approach, or both, he or she will be aiming to establish a knowledge of currency pairs' behavior and put up lucrative trades.

Forex trader symbols and currency market rates

In the 24-hour currency market, trading never sleeps, meaning there will always be movement, but forex liquidity levels will peak and dip at specific intervals throughout the clock. Some traders may desire to work at unsociable hours to put them in a position to gain on foreign markets.

WHAT IT TAKES TO BE AN EFFECTIVE FOREX TRADER, BY THE DAILYFX ANALYSTS

So what does it take to be an excellent forex trader? From holding a love for the markets to having the unbreakable discipline and more, here are the attributes that will aid you as a forex trader from the horse's mouth: our best analysts.

1) Have passion

"You must have a real interest - passion even - in whatever financial market/s you are going to trade"

When trading the foreign currency markets, you must have a serious interest and grasp of monetary policy, one of the key movers of price movement. For example, if you are trading GBP/USD you need to be totally in touch with both Bank of England and US Federal Reserve policy movements and speeches — both influence the market. So attempt to be on the same wavelength as the central bank/s, but don't gamble against them - they have large wallets and virtually always win.

2) Understand the macro drivers

"It's vitally important for traders to know that all currencies can have many macro drivers at any given point"

The Australian Dollar is a prominent example of a currency influenced by a variety of macro variables. It is typically conceived of as a 'growth' or 'risk' linked unit — one which is likely to thrive when the globe feels better about global growth and suffer when the contrary is the case. While this is frequently true, there are a great number of other plausible factors. Major commodity prices, Australian monetary policy expectations, and regional political risk may all see it go against the broader market grain at times.

In these days of highly interconnected markets, it's easy to split currencies into 'risk on' and 'risk off' camps but this is much too simple.

3) Remember: It takes two to forex tango

"Currency pairs are driven by both sides of the equation" When trading currencies, a trader has to comprehend what is occurring in both key areas. For example, while trading GBP/USD, it's good to stay up with the most current Brexit news in addition to the latest on the US/China trade war. More broadly, however, a thorough grasp of market trading is crucial, from stop losses to chart patterns; from market psychology to the function of central banks.

4) Exercise effective money management

"You can have the best forex trade ideas in the world and still lose if you can't limit losses and capture profits"

Sound money management is the essential distinction between the hobbyist and the skilled trader. To wit, genuine data from a prominent FX broker revealed that its customers closed EUR/USD transactions out at a gain 61% of the time, and yet lost money since the average winning trade was 48 pips while the average loss was 83 pips. That's no way to earn money, and that's precisely why money management is the difference between a hobbyist and a successful professional.

5) Have the appropriate mentality

"Strong self-discipline is needed to follow a clear-cut game plan"

You have to be a self-starter, able to hold yourself responsible and learn from your errors; there will be enough of them. A passion for markets and the act of trading, not simply money, is incredibly crucial - it will carry you through the hard times. Strong self-discipline is essential to follow a clear-cut game plan, but also the flexibility to adapt to changing situations since market conditions are continually altering.

6) Show grit

"Grit is highly underrated in most facets of life" Trading may be challenging. It can only look simple from the outside since clicking a few buttons to purchase or sell isn't extremely tough. But it's not simple to continually beat the herd, and practically anybody on this route will, at some time, confront hurdles. Grit is what permits success in those situations, and a lack of grit is what makes it easy to leave for whatever reason.

THE ULTIMATE CHECKLIST TO BECOME A FOREX TRADER

Now you know what attributes you need, it's time to grasp how to be a forex trader from a practical aspect. Here's the checklist:

1) Find a suitable broker

Choosing the finest forex broker will make all the difference when it comes to profiting from quality of user experience, trustworthy customer service, and affordable pricing.

2) Know how trading capital works

As a forex trader, you must understand margin and leverage. Margin permits a trader to establish leveraged positions, implying more exposure to the market with lower capital expenditure. Newer traders typically look at unused margins as purchasing power and hence tend to be excessively aggressive in their position size. Leverage boosts profits and losses making your account equity highly volatile. Regardless of the amount of leverage your broker provides, we advocate utilizing minimal or no leverage in your trading.

3) Start with a sample account

Practice using a demo account to acquaint yourself with the markets. From here, you may design and improve a trading strategy, become familiar with your chosen platform, and acquire the confidence you need to trade real money.

4) Take the plunge

Trade a little with your actual money account at the start, then work your way up. Trade with risk management measures in place, employing stop losses, and only trade after you have conducted an in-depth investigation, whether trading fundamentals or technicals, or both.

5) Never stop growing your knowledge – and character

Winning traders never stop learning and expanding their skills in major markets. You should know your preferred currency pairings inside out, which technical aspects are significant, and how market events impact the movements of various pairs. Recording your transactions in a trading notebook can help you measure your success and be in a position to regularly examine and reassess your strategy.

TRADING FOREX - WHAT I LEARNED

Trading forex is not a path to rapid cash. Excessive leverage might transform successful tactics into losing ones. Retail sentiment may operate as a potent trading filter. Everyone comes to the forex market for a purpose, ranging from merely for enjoyment to becoming a professional trader. I began off aiming to be a full-time, self-sufficient FX trader. I had been given the 'ideal' method. I spent months testing it and backtests revealed how I could generate $25,000-$35,000 a year off of a $10,000 account. My objective was to trade forex for a living and let my account compound until I was so well off, I wouldn't have to work again in my life. I was determined and I committed myself to the strategy 100%.

Sparing you the specifics, my strategy failed. It turns out that trading 300k lots on a $10,000 account is not very forgiving. I lost 20% of my money in three weeks. I didn't know what struck me. Something was wrong. Luckily, I quit trading at that moment and was lucky enough to obtain a position with a forex broker. I spent the following couple of years dealing with traders across the globe and proceeded to educate myself about the FX market. It had a major impact on my growth to be the trader I am today. Three years of lucrative trading later, it's been my pleasure to join the team at DailyFX and assist individuals to become successful or more successful traders.

The objective of my relaying this tale is because I believe many traders can relate to beginning out in this market, not getting the returns that they anticipated, and not understanding why. These are the three things I wish I had known before I began trading Forex.

1) Forex is not a get rich quick opportunity

Contrary to what you've heard on numerous pages throughout the web, Forex trading is not going to take your $10,000 account and transform it into $1 million. The amount we can make is governed more by the amount of money we are risking rather than how smart our approach is. The classic phrase "It takes money to make money" is a genuine one, Forex trading included.

But it doesn't imply it is not a good undertaking; after all, there are many successful Forex traders out there who trade for a livelihood. The difference is that they have progressively evolved over time and expanded their account to a level that can provide consistent revenue.

I hear about traders all the time seeking 50%, 60%, or 100% profit per year, or even per month, but the risk they are putting on is going to be quite close to the profit they are targeting. In other words, in order to strive to generate 60% profit in a year, it's not abnormal to see a loss of roughly 60% of your account in a given year.

"But Rob, I am trading with an edge, so I am not risking as much as I could potentially earn" you would respond. That's a true statement if you have a plan with a trading advantage.

Your predicted return should be positive, but without leverage, it is going to be a rather little sum. And during periods of terrible luck, we might still have losing streaks. When we bring leverage into the game, that's how traders aim to target those exorbitant profits. Which in turn is how traders might cause enormous losses. Leverage is advantageous up to point, but not when it may transform a winning approach into a loss.

2) Leverage can be a winning strategy to loosing money

This is a lesson I wish I had learned sooner. Excessive leverage may destroy an otherwise lucrative plan.

Let's imagine I had a coin that when heads were struck, you would gain $2, but when tails were hit, you would lose $1. Would you flip that coin? My hunch is that you would flip that coin. You'd want to turn it over and again. When you have a 50/50 chance between earning $2 or losing $1, it's a no-brainer option that you'd take.

Now let's pretend I had the same coin, but this time if heads were hit, you would treble your net worth; however, when tails were struck, you would lose every property you hold. Would you flip that coin? My assumption is you would not because one poor flip of the coin would wreck your life. Even if you have the exact same percentage edge in this scenario as the one before, no one in their right mind would flip this coin.

The second example is how many Forex traders perceive their trading accounts. They go "all-in" on one or two deals and wind up losing their whole account. Even if their transactions had an advantage like our coin-flipping example, it simply takes one or two unfortunate deals to wipe them out totally. This is how leverage may lead to a successful approach to losing money. So how can we remedy this? A solid start is by utilizing no more than 10x effective leverage.

3) Using sentiment as a guide can tilt the odds in your favor

The 3rd lesson I've learned should come as no surprise to those who follow my posts... utilizing the IG client sentiment tool (IGCS). It's the finest tool I've ever used and is still a component of practically every trading strategy I am utilizing current day.

IGCS is a free tool that informs us how many traders are long relative to how many traders are short each major currency pair. It's supposed to be utilized as a contrarian index where we want to do the opposite of what everyone else is doing. Using it as a direction filter for my transactions has turned my trading career entirely around.

LEARN FROM MY MISTAKES

If I could tell my younger self three things before I started trading forex, this would be the list I would provide. Ultimately Nevertheless, if you are just beginning out in the forex market, the greatest thing you can do is take time to study as much as you can, starting with the fundamentals. Read guidelines, stay up to speed with the newest news, and follow market experts on social media.

FOREX TRADING TIPS FREQUENTLY ASKED QUESTIONS (FAQ)

How much money can you earn trading Forex?

Due to the availability of leverage, forex traders may generate a return on a single deal that is multiples of the margin they needed to start the trade. However, leverage is a double-edged sword in that high profits may also bring significant losses. Therefore, dependence on excessive leverage as a strategy often leads to the destruction of your account capital over the long term. This is because it just takes one unfavorable market move to push the market far enough and trigger severe losses.

Your expectations on a return on investment are a vital part. When traders demand too much from their accounts, they depend on excessive leverage and it often causes a losing account over time. View forex as you would any other market and anticipate regular profits by employing prudent quantities of no leverage.

Since forex is a 24-hour market, the flexibility of trading depending on your availability makes it popular among day traders, swing traders, and part-time traders. Regardless of your style, employ tiny (if any) levels of leverage.

If you were to extend the list to a fourth item learned while beginning to trade FX, what would it be?

I touched on leverage above. We examined millions of live transactions and summarized our findings in a Traits of Successful Traders guide. In the guide we touch on risk-to-reward ratios and how it is significant. With people being human, we also touch on the psychological factor that goes along with trading and why we may still make terrible decisions even though we know what is correct. Sometimes our largest challenge is between our ears.

Forex trading, which is the act of exchanging fiat currencies, is estimated to be millennia old - reaching back to the Babylonian era. Today, the forex market is one of the largest, most liquid, and accessible marketplaces in the world, and has been influenced by various key global events, such as Bretton Woods and the gold standard.

It's crucial for forex traders to grasp the history of forex trading, and the main historical events which have formed the market. This is because identical occurrences might certainly occur again in different, but similar forms - influencing the trade environment. History tends to repeat itself.

HISTORY OF FOREX TRADING: WHERE IT ALL BEGAN

The barter system is the earliest means of commerce and originated around 6000 BC, brought by Mesopotamian tribes. Under the barter system products were swapped for other goods. The system eventually developed and items like salt and spices became prominent means of trade. Ships would sail to barter for these items in the first known form of international currency. Eventually, as early as the 6th century BC, the first gold coins were manufactured, and they worked as money since they possessed key features including mobility, durability, divisibility, uniformity, limited supply, and acceptance.

Gold coins were generally recognized as a means of commerce, but they were impractical since they were heavy. In the 1800s nations embraced the gold standard. The gold standard ensured that the government would redeem any quantity of paper money for its worth in gold. This functioned great until World War I as European nations had to suspend the gold standard to create additional money to pay for the war.

The foreign currency market was underpinned by the gold standard at this moment and throughout the early 1900s. Countries traded with each other because they could turn the money they received into gold. The gold standard, however, could not hold up throughout the global wars.

KEY EVENTS THAT HAVE SHAPED THE FOREX MARKET

Throughout history, we have witnessed big events that have substantially altered the currency trading market. Here are some highlights:

Timeline outlining the history of FX since the 1800s
The Bretton Woods System 1944 – 1971

Sign representing the Bretton Woods monetary conference
The first significant alteration of the foreign currency market, the Bretton Woods System, happened around the close of World War II. The United States, Great Britain, and France convened at the United Nations Monetary and

Financial Conference in Bretton Woods, NH to build a new global economic system. The area was selected because, at the time, the US was the only nation untouched by war. Most of the major European nations were in disarray. In reality, WWII propelled the US dollar from a failing currency following the stock market crisis of 1929 to a benchmark currency by which most other foreign currencies were evaluated.

The Bretton Woods Accord was created to provide a stable atmosphere under which world economies could rebuild themselves. It tried this by developing an adjustable pegged foreign exchange market. An adjustable pegged exchange rate is an exchange rate regime wherein a currency is linked to another currency. In this instance, other nations would 'fix' their currency rate to the US Dollar. The US currency was being linked to gold, since the US owned the biggest gold reserves in the world at that time. So other nations would deal in the US Dollar (this is also how the US dollar became the world's reserve currency).

The Bretton Woods agreement finally failed to peg gold to the US currency because there was not enough gold to support the quantity of US Dollars in circulation since the amount of US Dollars in circulation expanded owing to rising government financing and spending. In 1971, President Richard M. Nixon abandoned the Bretton Woods arrangement which quickly led to the free-floating of the US Dollar against other foreign currencies.

The Beginning of the Free-Floating System

After the Bretton Woods Accord followed the Smithsonian Agreement in December of 1971, which was similar but allowed for a larger fluctuation band for the currencies. The United States tied the dollar to gold at $38/ounce, effectively devaluing the currency. Under the Smithsonian agreement, other major currencies might vary by 2.25% against the US Dollar, while the US Dollar was fixed to gold.

In 1972, the European community strove to shift away from its dependence on the US Dollar. The European Joint Float was then founded by West Germany, France, Italy, the Netherlands, Belgium, and Luxemburg. Both accords committed flaws like the Bretton Woods Accord and in 1973 disintegrated. These failures culminated in an official move to the free-floating system.

The Plaza Accord

In the early 1980s, the dollar had risen substantially versus the other major currencies. This was severe for exporters and the US current account subsequently had a deficit of 3.5% of GDP. In reaction to stagflation that started in the early 1980s, Paul Volcker hiked interest rates which generated a strong US Dollar (and lowered inflation) at the price of the US industry's competitiveness in the worldwide market.

The weight of the US currency was burying third-world countries under debt and shutting American manufacturing because they could not compete with overseas competition. In 1985, the G-5, the most powerful economies in the world – the US, Great Britain, France, West Germany, and Japan – sent officials to what was intended to be a secret summit at the Plaza Hotel in New York City. News of the meeting leaked, leading the G-5 to release a statement promoting the appreciation of non-dollar currencies. This became known as the "Plaza Accord" and its reverberations prompted a dramatic collapse in the currency.

It did not take long for traders to discover the possibilities for profit in this new realm of currency trading. Even with government interference, there remained substantial degrees of volatility, and where there is variation, there is profit. This became obvious a little over a decade after the fall of Bretton Woods.

Establishment of the Euro

Euro banknotes in denominations of 50
After WWII, Europe formed various accords meant to bring nations of the continent closer together. None were more productive than the 1992 accord known as the Maastricht accord, named after the Dutch city where the meeting was place. The treaty founded the European Union (EU), led to the development of the Euro currency, and put together a coherent whole that included measures on foreign policy and security. The treaty has been modified multiple times, but the introduction of the Euro afforded European banks and companies the particular advantage of reducing exchange risk in an ever-globalized economy.

Internet Trading

In the 1990s, the currency markets became more complex and quicker than ever because money – and how people saw and used it – was changing. An individual sitting alone at home may discover, with the touch of a mouse, a precise price that just a few years before would have needed an army of traders, brokers, and telephones. These advancements in communication happened at a period when old divides gave way to capitalism and globalization (the collapse of the Berlin Wall and the Soviet Union).

For forex, everything changed. Currencies that were previously cut off in authoritarian political regimes might be exchanged. Emerging economies, such as those in Southeast Asia, prospered, drawing cash and currency speculation.

The history of FX markets since 1944 shows a typical illustration of a free market in operation. Competitive forces have produced a marketplace with exceptional liquidity. Spreads have reduced considerably with greater online competition among trustworthy players. Individuals trading big sums now have access to the same electronic communications networks used by multinational banks and merchants.

Today, the forex market is the biggest market in the world. More than $5 trillion is transacted on the FX market every day. The future of forex is clouded in ambiguity and is constantly changing, resulting in eternal chances for forex traders.

FOREX MARKET SIZE TALKING POINTS:

The FX market is the biggest and most liquid market in the world. The US dollar makes up the bulk of FX transactions. The forex market's tremendous liquidity is favorable to traders by enabling them to join and leave the market immediately. The scale and depth of the FX market make it an attractive trading market. Its liquidity makes it easier for dealers to sell and purchase currencies without delay. This provides narrow spreads for positive quotations. Low costs, vast scope to multiple markets, and flexible trading periods make it the most commonly traded market in the world. This essay will explain the immensity of the forex market, which allows for a better grasp of the mechanics underlying it on a macro scale. Ultimately offering a strong basis for forex trading for novices up to professional traders.

HOW BIG IS THE FOREX MARKET AND HOW MUCH IS IT WORTH?

According to the Bank for International Settlements triennial report of 2016, the foreign currency market cap averaged $5.1 trillion per day. This value is down from the prior estimate in 2013 of $5.4 trillion. There are just a handful of nations that account for the bulk of forex trading turnover.

From a trader's standpoint, huge forex market capitalization lends to less volatility since large deals do not have as substantial influence on the price of the market. Smaller markets may be impacted by huge institutions/traders with relative ease, yet within the FX market this effect is comparably diluted.

The FX market is made of numerous important parts. The most influential being banks. The interbank market covers the highest amount of foreign exchange trade inside the currency area. This involves trading between banks, transactions for customers, and facilitated trading by their separate desks. The US banks hold the biggest portion of this market. Central banks, investment managers, hedge funds, businesses, and ultimately individual traders round up the remainder of the market. Roughly 90% of this volume is created by currency speculators profiting on intraday price changes.

As retail traders, it is necessary to appreciate the immensity of the forex market to be successful in your trading strategy, as well as how these distinct components interact with each other on a wider scale.

FOREX TRADING VOLUME

Traders from other markets are drawn to forex due to its extraordinarily high degree of liquidity. Liquidity is vital since it enables traders to get in and out of a position with ease 24 hours a day, five and a half days a week. It permits big trading volumes to enter and leave the market without the significant changes in price that would happen in a less liquid market. This indicates that you will never be in a position due to the absence of a buyer. This liquidity might change from one trading session to another and one currency pair to another as well.

As the most traded currency pairings, EUR/USD and USD/JPY account for around 41% of all forex trading yearly. This is an incredible number given the enormity of the global forex market size. Another interesting aspect is that most of the pairings represented in the graphic below are USD crosses.

The US Dollar takes nearly 85% of forex trading volume. At approximately 40% of trade volume, the Euro is ahead of the third-place Japanese Yen which gets about 20%. With volume focused predominantly on the US Dollar, Euro, and Yen, forex traders may focus their attention on just a handful of significant pairings. In addition, the increased liquidity present in the forex market is favorable to extended, well-defined trends that react well to technical analysis and charting approaches.

HOW TO TAKE ADVANTAGE OF THE FOREX MARKET

Traders wanting to profit from the benefits that come with the sheer size and volume of the forex market need to assess what approach or combination of analysis matches their trading style. At a basic level, traders need to grasp the key pillars of forex trading:

- Fundamental Analysis: Since currencies move in a market, you may look at supply and demand. This is termed basic analysis. Interest rates, economic growth, employment, inflation, and political risk are all variables that might impact supply and demand for currencies.

- Technical Analysis: Price charts tell numerous tales and most forex traders rely on them in making their trading choices. Charts may show out patterns and critical price points where traders can join or leave the market, assuming you know how to interpret them.

- Money Management: A crucial component of trading. All traders need to know how to estimate their possible risks and returns and use this to determine entrances, exits, and transaction size. Forex traders utilize these pillars in varied ways to develop a strategy they are comfortable with. Once they discover a balance between these core systems, they will switch their focus to specializing and sharpening their talents by staying up to speed with politics, monetary/fiscal policies etc., and making educated judgments based on the facts at hand. A technical trader may employ numerous indicators/drawings and conduct trades resulting from these technical indications. Client emotion may also provide forex traders an inside scoop as to anticipated reversals, market-entry, and exit locations. Join our monthly Trading Sentiment webinar, or check our live IG client sentiment report for more details.

DIFFERENCE BETWEEN FOREX & STOCK

Traders typically analyze forex vs. stocks to decide which market is best to trade. Despite being intertwined, the FX and stock market are radically distinct. The forex market has distinct qualities that set it different from other markets, and in the view of many, also make it considerably more enticing to trade.

When deciding to trade forex or stocks, it frequently boils down to determining which trading style fits you best. But recognizing the distinctions and similarities between the stock and forex market also assists traders in making educated trading choices based on aspects such as market conditions, liquidity, and volume.

TOP 5 DIFFERENCES BETWEEN FOREX AND STOCKS

Let's take a more in-depth look at how precisely the FX market compares with equities (stocks).

1) Volume

One of the main contrasts between forex and stocks is the sheer scale of the forex market. Forex is expected to trade over $5 trillion a day, with most trading centered on a few big pairings including the EUR/USD, USD/JPY, GBP/USD, and AUD/USD. The forex market volume eclipses the dollar volume of all the world's stock exchanges combined, which average around $200 billion each day.

Having such a big trading volume might provide various benefits to traders. High volume implies traders can often have their orders completed more easily and closer to the pricing they seek. While all markets are prone to gaps, having greater liquidity at each price point better prepares traders to join and leave the market.

2) Liquidity

A market that trades in great volume often has high liquidity. Liquidity leads to narrower spreads and reduced transaction costs. Forex main pairs often have exceptionally low spreads and transactions costs when compared to stocks and this is one of the primary benefits of trading the forex market over trading the stock market. Read more about the variations in liquidity between the currency and the stock market.

3) 24 Hour Markets

Forex is an over-the-counter market meaning that it is not conducted via a standard exchange. Trading is enabled via the interbank market. This implies that trading may take on all across the globe throughout various nations' business hours and trading sessions. Therefore, the forex trader has access to trading almost 24 hours a day, 5 days a week. Major stock indexes, on the other hand, trade at various periods and are impacted by diverse factors. Visit the Major Indices website to find out more about trading these markets-including information on trading hours.

4) Minimal or no commission

Most forex brokers charge no fee, instead, they earn their margin on the spread - which is the difference between the purchase price and the selling price. When trading equities (stocks) a futures contract, or a large index like the S&P 500, frequently traders must pay the spread along with a fee to a broker.

Forex spreads are fairly clear compared to the expenses of trading other contracts. Below you will see the spread of the EUR/USD highlighted inside of the executable trading rates. The spread may be used to compute the cost for your position size upfront before to execution.

5) Narrow focus versus broad focus

There are eight main currencies traders may concentrate on, but in the stock world, there are hundreds. With just eight economies to concentrate on and as forex is traded in pairs, traders will search for diverging and converging patterns between the currencies to match up a forex pair to trade. Eight currencies are simpler to keep an eye on than thousands of other Stocks. The factors that impact the main currencies may be readily tracked using an economic calendar.

Should you trade forex or stocks?

Whether you opt to trade forex or stocks relies significantly on your objectives and chosen trading style.

Different sorts of trading styles

Short- Term Trading (Scalping)

A trading method where the trader attempts to initiate and complete deals within minutes, taking advantage of tiny price fluctuations. Traders might concentrate more on volatility and less on fundamental issues that drive the market. As a consequence of making more trades, beginning traders may lose more money if their technique isn't fine-tuned. Suited to forex trading owing to affordable expenses of executing trades. Some exchanges demand substantial capital account balances to trade. Most forex brokers merely ask you to have enough cash to sustain the margin requirements.

Medium-Term Trading

A trading technique where the trader seeks to maintain positions for one or more days, where the trades are generally launched due to technical factors.
Lower capital needs compared with other types since a trader is searching for greater swings. Trades must be coupled by analysis which may take time.

Long-Term Trading

A trading technique where a trader attempts to maintain positions for months or years, frequently basing choices on long-term fundamental considerations.

Traders do not have to spend as much time analyzing. Large capital needs necessary to cover volatility changes.

Suited better to stock trading since the currency market tends to change in direction more than stocks.

FOREX VS. OTHER MARKETS FAQS

How can I switch from forex trading to stock trading?

To shift from forex to stock trading you will need to grasp the basic distinctions between forex and stocks. When you break it down, FX fluctuations are triggered by interest rates and their projected changes. Stocks are depending on revenue, balance sheet predictions, and the economies they operate in amongst other factors. Find out more about how to shift from FX to stock trading.

Are there any distinctions between forex and commodities trading?

Forex and commodities vary in terms of regulation, leverage, and exchange limitations. Forex markets are a lot less regulated than commodities markets whereas commodities markets are heavily controlled. In terms of leverage, it exists in both the forex and commodities markets, but in the currency market, it is more common owing to better liquidity and reduced volatility (leverage may multiply losses and profits).

Also, like stocks, commodities trade on exchanges. Commodity exchanges establish ceilings and floors for the price variations of commodities and when these limitations are reached trading may be suspended for a limited period depending on the commodity traded. The currency and stock market do not have constraints that may prohibit trade from occurring.

Forex quotations indicate the price of various currencies at any moment in time. Since a trader's profit or loss is decided by swings in price (the quotation), it is vital to gain a strong knowledge of how to interpret currency pairings.

WHAT ARE FOREX QUOTES?

A forex quotation is the price of one currency in terms of another currency. These rates usually contain currency pairings since you are purchasing one currency by selling another. For example, the price of one Euro may cost $1.1404 when examining the EUR/USD currency combination. Brokers will normally offer two prices for every currency pair and get the difference (spread) between the two prices, under normal market circumstances.

The next sections will elaborate on the distinct features of a forex quotation. The same quotation will be used throughout this post to keep the figures constant.

UNDERSTANDING FOREX QUOTE BASICS

In order to interpret currency pairings accurately, traders need to be aware of the following fundamentals of a forex quote:

- ISO code: The Worldwide Organization for Standardization (ISO) establishes and publishes worldwide standards and has applied this to global currencies. This implies each country's currency is shortened to three letters. For example, the Euro is abbreviated to EUR and the US dollar to USD.

- Base currency and variable currency: Forex quotations display two currencies, the base currency, which comes first, and the quote or variable currency, which appears last. The price of the first currency is always represented in units of the second currency. Sticking with the preceding EUR/USD example, it is plain to see that one Euro will cost one dollar, 14 cents, and 04 pips. This is strange since you cannot physically keep fractions of one cent yet this is a typical aspect of the foreign currency market.

BID AND ASK PRICE

When trading forex, a currency pair will always quote two separate rates as seen below:

The bid (SELL) price is the price at which traders can sell currency, and the ask (purchase) price is the price at which traders may purchase currency. This may seem perplexing since it is only natural to think of "bid" in terms of purchasing so just remember the bid/ask language is from the broker's viewpoint.

Traders will constantly be aiming to purchase forex when the price is low and sell when the price increases; or sell forex in the expectation that the currency will decline and buy it back at a cheaper price in the future.

SPREADS The price to acquire a currency will often be greater than the price to sell the currency. This difference is called the spread and is where the broker gets money for completing the deal. Spreads tend to be narrower (smaller) for big currency pairings owing to their large trading volume and liquidity. The EUR/USD is the most actively traded currency pair, thus it is no surprise that the spread, in this case, is 0.6 pips.

Quotes are sometimes provided in accordance with the "home currency" in mind i.e. the nation you live in. A direct quotation for traders in the US, wishing to purchase Euros, will read EUR/USD and will be relevant to US residents since the quote is in USD. This straight quotation will offer US residents the price of one Euro, in terms of their local currency which is 1.1404.

The indirect quotation is simply the opposite of the direct currency (1/direct quote = 0.8769). It indicates the value of one unit of local currency in terms of foreign currency. Indirect quotations might be beneficial to convert foreign currency purchases overseas into home currency.

TOP TIPS TO READ FOREX QUOTES

Bid and Ask pricing are from the standpoint of the broker. Traders purchase currencies at the asking price and sell at the bid price. The base currency is the first currency in the pair and the quote currency is the second currency. The lowest fluctuation for non-JPY currency pairings is one pip (a single-digit movement in the fourth decimal place of the quoted price and a single-digit movement in the second decimal place for JPY pairs). The spread is the first obstacle (cost) that traders realize in a deal.

When it comes to buying and selling forex, traders have various methods and techniques. This is because the forex market is one of the most liquid and biggest in the world and as a consequence, there is no one unique strategy to trade.

Knowing when to buy and sell forex relies on several aspects, but there tends to be greater volume when markets are volatile because of the accompanying increased risk. This book will discuss the idea of buying and selling currencies using practical examples as well as extra resources to increase your forex trading expertise.

WHAT IT MEANS TO BUY AND SELL FOREX

Buying and selling forex pairs entails evaluating the appreciation/depreciation in value of one currency versus the other. This might incorporate fundamental or technical analysis as a basis of the transaction. Once a base has been built, the trader will turn to additional technical and fundamental variables. Key stages of admission and departure will follow, bearing in mind risk management protocols.

FACTORS WHICH AFFECT CURRENCY PAIRS

Political events

administration instability, corruption, and changes in administration may alter the value of a currency - for example, when President Donald Trump was elected the Dollar skyrocketed in value!

Economic policy

From a basic aspect, forex traders keep a careful check on unemployment data, GDP, and monetary and fiscal policies (just to mention a few) which have an impact on the value of currencies. Our economic calendar indicates impending events which may shake up the financial markets.

Technical analysis

Technical traders prefer to emphasize important price levels (support & resistance), trends and other indications to establish a foundation for their forex transactions.

HOW TO BUY AND SELL EUR/USD

Using the EUR/USD currency pair, we will present an example of how and when to purchase or sell forex. Let's assume you want to purchase the EUR/USD. If the EUR rises higher in value compared to the USD after the deal is sold, you might have earned a profit (depending on commission and other expenses). A trader in this case would be purchasing the EUR and selling the USD at the same time. As an example, if the EUR/USD pair was purchased at 11300 and the pair went up to 11504 at the time that the trade was closed/exited, the profit on the transaction would have been 204 pips.

- Entry level - The morning star candlestick pattern provides a probable entry point, which was verified by the usage of the RSI indicator which exhibits an oversold signal.

- Exit level — Using important price levels to determine first take profit level.

Similarly, a fundamental trader might trade the USD/JPY currency pair by tracking political and economic developments. For example, if a fundamental trader anticipated the Fed to boost interest rates, this may draw higher foreign investment into the US, and hence more demand for the domestic currency (USD). The trader might then try to engage in a long (buy) position in expectation of the USD to appreciate in value. Of course, this is not totally definite since economic principles/theory do not always correspond to actual world realities. Taking short positions on forex pairs is significantly more sophisticated as compared to purchasing. Read more about how to short forex to acquire additional information.

UNDERSTANDING RISK MANAGEMENT WHEN BUYING AND SELLING FOREX

Risk management is crucial to longevity in forex trading. This does not merely involve a favorable risk/reward ratio but comprehending the possible swings in volatility as well. Factors impacting forex pairings may have considerable effects at times therefore avoiding unwanted consequences on your transaction can be handled by using correct risk management measures. Buying and selling forex may be difficult, thus knowing the mechanics behind it, such as how to interpret currency pairings, is necessary before making a deal. We also suggest reading our forex guide for beginners to obtain a crash education on the fundamentals of forex trading.

Understanding the fundamentals of going long or short in forex is crucial for all new traders. Taking a long or short position boils down to whether a trader believes a currency will appreciate (go up) or depreciate (go down), compared to another currency. Simply stated, when a trader believes a currency will gain they will "Go Long" the underlying currency, and when the trader anticipates the currency to devalue they will "Go Short" the underlying currency. Keep reading to find out more about long and short positions in forex trading and when to utilize them.

<u>WHAT IS A POSITION IN FOREX TRADING?</u>

A forex position is the quantity of a currency that is held by a person or company that subsequently has exposure to the fluctuations of the currency versus other currencies. The position might be either short or lengthy. A forex position has three characteristics:

- The underlying currency pair
- The direction (long or short)
- The size

Traders may take positions in multiple currency pairings. If they predict the price of the currency to appreciate, they might go long. The amount of the stake they take would depend on their account equity and margin needs. It is crucial that traders employ the right level of leverage.

WHAT DOES IT MEAN TO HAVE A LONG OR SHORT POSITION IN FOREX?

Having a long or short position in forex involves betting on a currency pair to either go up or go down in value. Going long or short is the most essential facet of dealing with the markets. When a trader goes long, he or she will have a positive investment balance in an asset, with the belief the asset would appreciate. When short, he or she will have a negative investment balance, with the intention that the asset would decline so it can be purchased back at a reduced price in the future.

WHAT IS A LONG POSITION AND WHEN TO TRADE IT?

A long position is an executed deal where the trader anticipates the underlying instrument to appreciate. For example, when a trader executes a purchase order, they hold a long position in the underlying asset they bought i.e. USD/JPY. Here they are anticipating the US Dollar to appreciate versus the Japanese Yen.

For example, a trader who has acquired two lots of USD/JPY has a long position of two lots in USD/JPY. The underlying is the USD/JPY, the direction is long, and the amount is two lots. Traders search for buy signals to initiate long positions. Indicators are employed by traders to seek to buy and sell indications to join the market.

An example of a buy signal is when a currency falls to a level of support. In the chart below USD/JPY depreciates to 110.274 but is sustained at that level many times. This level of 110.274 becomes a support level and provides traders a buy signal for when the price descends to that level.

USDJPY slides to a support level presenting a buy signal for traders. A benefit of the FX market is that it trades almost 24/5. Some traders prefer to trade during the big trading sessions like the New York session, the London session, and occasionally the Sydney and Tokyo session since there is greater liquidity.

WHAT IS A SHORT POSITION AND WHEN TO TRADE IT?

A short position is simply the reverse of a long position. When traders initiate a short position, they anticipate the price of the underlying currency to devalue (go down). To short a currency implies selling the underlying currency in the anticipation that its price will go down in the future, enabling the trader to purchase the same currency back at a later period but at a lower price. The difference between the higher selling price and the lower purchase price is profit. To offer a realistic example, if a trader shorts USD/JPY, they are selling USD to purchase JPY.

Traders search for sell signals to initiate short bets. A frequent sell-signal is when the price of the underlying currency hits for level of resistance. A level of resistance is a price level that the underlying has failed to break above. In the chart below USD/JPY appreciates to 114.486 and struggles to appreciate further. This level becomes a resistance level and provides traders with a sell signal when the price reaches 114.486.

USDJPY reaches for resistance presenting a sell signal for traders
Some traders choose to trade just during the big trading sessions, yet if an opportunity presents itself, traders may execute their deal almost whenever the forex market is open.

<u>WHAT ARE PIPS IN FOREX TRADING?</u>

A "PIP" – which stands for Point in Percentage - is the unit of measure used by forex traders to represent the smallest change in value between two currencies. This is indicated as a single-digit change in the fourth decimal position in a typical forex quotation.

For example, if the price of EUR/USD changes from 1.1402 to 1.1403 this would be one pip or 'point' shift.

Example of a pip using the quotation to purchase EUR/USD

A pip on a EUR/USD quotation to purchase EUR/USD
However, not all currency rates are shown in this fashion, with the Japanese Yen being the prominent exception. Keep reading to find out more about pips and how they're employed in forex trading, with examples from chosen main currency pairings.

HOW TO CALCULATE THE VALUE OF A PIP?

The pip value is obtained by multiplying one pip (0.0001) by the relevant lot/contract size. For regular lots this comprises 100,000 units of the basic currency and for micro lots, this is 10,000 units. For example, looking at EUR/USD, a one-pip movement in a normal contract is equivalent to $10 (0.0001 x 100 000).

Being able to quantify the value of a single pip helps forex traders put a monetary value to their take profit goals and stop loss levels. Instead of just evaluating fluctuations in pips, traders may predict how the value of their trading account (equity) will alter when the currency market moves.

It's vital to realize that the value of one pip will change for various currency pairings. This is because the value of one pip will always be presented in the currency of the quote/variable currency and this will change when trading various currency pairings. When trading EUR/USD, the value of one pip will be represented in USD, when trading GBP/JPY, this will be in JPY.

CALCULATING THE VALUE OF ONE PIP - EUR/USD PIPS EXAMPLE

As each currency has its own relative value, it is required to compute the value of a pip for each individual currency pair.

Keep in mind that forex trading includes specific quantities of currency that you may exchange. Most brokers provide a standard and a micro contract with the parameters in the table below:

Standard Lot 100 000 Mini Lot 10 000
The value of one pip for the EUR/USD standard contract is computed as follows:

- Pip Value = Contract Size x One Pip

- Pip Value = 100 000 x 0.0001

- Pip Value = $10

Every one pip move in your favor translates into a $10 profit and every one pip move that goes against you translates into a $10 loss. By the same reasoning, a one-pip move in a micro contract converts into a $1 profit or loss (10,000 x 0.0001).

To better understand pips and pip calculations even further you may want to try conducting some practice calculations on your own.

PIP VALUE CONVERSIONS

Now, if your account is based in Great British Pounds (GBP), you would have to convert that $1 (worth of a pip for a 10k EUR/USD lot) into Pounds. To do so, merely divide the $1 by the current GBP/USD exchange rate, which at the time of writing is 1.2863. It is vital to divide here since a Pound is worth more than a US dollar, thus I know my answer should be less than 1. 1 divided by 1.2863 equals 0.7774 Pounds. So now you know that if you have a Pound-based account, you profit or lose one pip on one 10k lot of EUR/USD, you will gain or lose 0.7774 Pounds.

THE EXCEPTION - USD/JPY PIPS

When trading major currencies against the Japanese Yen, traders need to remember that a pip is no longer the fourth decimal but rather the second decimal. This is because the Japanese Yen has a significantly lower value than the main currencies.

Looking at the USD/JPY quotation below, the ask (buy) price is as high as 107.99 Yen for 1 USD.

USD/JPY pips explained in a forex trading quotation

When trading the micro contracts (10k) and regular contracts (100k) in Japanese Yen, a one-pip movement (the value of one pip) will be JPY100 and JPY1000, respectively.

There's a substantial association between interest rates and FX trading. Forex is regulated by numerous elements, but the interest rate of the currency is the basic aspect that triumphs above them all.

Simply stated, money seeks to follow the currency with the greatest real interest rate. The real interest rate is the nominal interest rate minus inflation.

Forex traders must keep a watch on each country's central bank interest rate and more critically, when it is projected to change, to predict swings in currencies.

WHAT ARE INTEREST RATES AND WHY DO THEY MATTER TO FOREX TRADERS?

When traders speak about 'interest rates' they are generally referring to central bank interest rates. Interest rates are of vital significance to forex traders because when the predicted rate of interest rates changes, the currency often follows with it. The central bank has numerous monetary policy instruments it may employ to modify the interest rate. The most prevalent being:

- Open market operations: The buying and selling of securities in the market with the objective of affecting interest rates.

- The discount rate: The rate paid to commercial banks and other depository institutions on loans they receive from their regional Federal Reserve Bank's lending facility.

- Central banks have two key tasks: To regulate inflation and create stability for their country's currency rate. They achieve this by altering interest rates and controlling the nation's money supply. When inflation is creeping higher, over the central bank's objective, they will boost the central bank rate (using the policy instruments) which may constrain the economy and put inflation back in control.

- The economic cycle and interest rates: Economies are either growing or declining. When economies are flourishing, everyone is better off, and when economies are shrinking (recession) they are worse off. The central bank strives to keep inflation in line while enabling the economy to develop at a reasonable pace, all by adjusting the interest rate.

- When economies are growing (GDP Growth positive), consumers start to earn more: More income leads to more spending, which leads to more money chasing fewer products - generating inflation. If inflation is allowed uncontrolled it may be terrible, thus the central bank strives to limit inflation at its goal level, which is 2% (for most central banks), by raising interest rates. Increased interest rates make borrowing costlier and help limit expenditure and inflation.

- If the economy is declining (GDP growth negative), deflation (negative inflation) becomes an issue: The central bank reduces interest rates to promote consumption and investment. Companies start to loan money at low-interest rates to invest in projects, which generates employment, growth, and eventually inflation.

HOW DO INTEREST RATES AFFECT CURRENCIES?

The way interest rates affect the forex markets is via a change in expectations of interest rates that leads to a change in demand for the currency. The table below depicts the potential possibilities that emerge from a change in interest rate expectations:

Rate Hike Rate Hold Depreciation of currency Rate Cut Rate Hold Appreciation of currency Rate Hold Rate Hike Appreciation of currency Rate Hold Rate Cut Depreciation of currency Interest rate importance to FX trading

Imagine you are an investor in the UK that has to invest a substantial quantity of money in a risk-free asset, such as a government bond. Interest rates in the US are on the increase therefore you start to acquire US Dollars to invest in US government bonds.

You (being the UK investor) are not alone in investing in the nation with higher interest rates. Many other investors follow the rise in yield and thus raise the demand for US Dollars which appreciates the currency. This is the core of how interest rates affect currencies. Traders might try to foresee changes in expectations of the interest rate which can have a major influence on the currency.

Here is an example of what occurs when the market expects the central bank to maintain interest rates on hold, but then the central bank cuts the interest rate. In this case, the Reserve Bank of Australia was anticipated to maintain interest rates on hold at 2% but instead dropped them to 1.75%. The market was stunned by the rate drop therefore the AUD/USD fell.

UNDERSTANDING FOREX INTEREST RATE DIFFERENTIALS

Interest rate differentials are essentially disparities in interest rates between two nations.

If a trader expects the US to suddenly boost interest rates he/she predicts the US dollar may rise. To boost the trader's chances of success, the trader may purchase the US Dollar against a currency with low-interest rates while the two currencies are diverging in the direction of their respective interest rates.

Interest rates and their differentials have a substantial effect on the appreciation/depreciation of the currency pair. The changes in interest rate differentials are associated with the appreciation/depreciation of the currency pair. It is simpler to grasp visually. The chart below shows the AUD/USD currency pair (candlestick graph) with the difference between the two-year AUD government bonds and the two-year USD government bonds (orange graph). The link indicates that when the AUD bond yield drops compared to the USD bonds, so does the currency.

AUD/USD contrasted with 2-year AUD/USD rate disparity

Interest rate differentials are extensively employed in carry trading. In a carry trade money is lent from a nation with a low rate and invested in a country with a higher interest rate. There are, however, dangers inherent with the carry trade such as the currency invested falling compared to the currency used for financing the deal.

HOW TO FORECAST CENTRAL BANK RATES AND THE IMPACT ON FX MARKETS

Fed funds futures are contracts traded on the Chicago Mercantile Exchange (CME) that indicate the market's expectations of where the daily official federal funds rate will be when the contract expires. The market always has its own projection of where the interest rate will be. A trader's task is to foresee a shift in those expectations.

For a trader to anticipate central bank rates he/she will need to keep a close watch on what the central bankers are now observing. Central bankers aim to be as honest as possible to the public about when they intend to raise interest rates and which economic indicators they are presently reviewing.

The central bankers decide to boost or reduce interest rates depending on many economic data factors. You can remain up to current with the publication of these data points using an economic calendar. Inflation, unemployment, and the exchange rate are some of the important data indicators. The trader must be in touch with the central bank policymakers and nearly attempt to foresee what their actions will be before they disclose it to the public. In this manner, the trader may enjoy the rewards of the market's shift in expectations. This style of trading is based on the fundamentals which are distinct from trading utilizing technical analysis. See our post on Technical versus Fundamental analysis to learn the various approaches to evaluate forex.

FOREX INTEREST RATE TRADING STRATEGIES

Forex traders might elect to trade the consequence of the interest rate news release, purchasing or selling the currency the instant the news breaks. See our guide on trading the news for additional professional insight.

Advanced forex traders may seek to foresee changes in central banker's tones, which may influence market expectations. Traders will accomplish this by monitoring important economic metrics like inflation, and trade before the central banker's statements. See our Central Bank WeeklyWebinar for professional analysis of the recent and impending central bank decisions.

Another option is to wait for a downturn in the currency pair following the interest rate outcome. If the central bank suddenly boosts rates, the currency should appreciate, and a trader may wait for the currency to decline before executing a buy position- assuming that the currency would continue to rise.

The interest rate choices themselves tend to be less influential than the expectations for future interest changes.

Trading currencies with larger interest rate differentials might boost the chance of successful deals.

It is crucial to remain up to speed with economic data using an economic calendar to foresee prospective changes in market expectations.